SERIES: Freedom Price Tag

Book One: The Journey Between Two Worlds

A true story of origins, identity, and the first cost of freedom

By

Anonymous

The Journey Between Two Worlds

Book One of the Freedom Price Tag Series

by

An Anonymous Author

Freedom is never free—but it is always worth the price.

First Edition
Printed in the United States of America

ISBN: 979-8-9950520-0-5

Author's Note

This book is written anonymously by choice.

Not out of fear—but out of intention.

These pages hold a true story. A life shaped by migration, faith, endurance, and the cost of choosing freedom again and again. Some names, locations, and identifying details have been changed—not to soften the truth, but to protect those who did not choose to carry it publicly.

This story is not written in anger, nor as an act of exposure. It is written in clarity.

I believe deeply in accountability—but also in peace. I believe in telling the truth without turning it into a weapon. And I believe that silence, when chosen consciously, can be an act of strength.

My hope is simple: that someone, somewhere, will recognize themselves in these pages and understand that survival does not mean the end of joy—and that starting over is not failure, but courage.

This is not a story about blame.
It is a story about becoming.

Series Note

Freedom Price Tag is a four-book memoir series chronicling a life shaped by migration, faith, resilience, and the cost of choosing oneself.

Book I – The Journey Between Two Worlds

Origins, childhood, and the first rupture.

Book II – The Bridge to Freedom

Displacement, survival, and the slow construction of independence.

Book III – Breaking Free

Recognition, endurance, and the price of staying too long.

Book IV – Flying Free

Action, survival, betrayal, and a hard-won arrival.

Each book represents a distinct psychological passage—together forming a single arc from endurance to sovereignty.

Table of Contents

Prologue

The city stretches endlessly beyond the glass, drowned in the molten gold of an autumn dusk. For a heartbeat, I stand still—caught between who I was and who I am about to become. The wind hums against the windowpane, restless and alive, echoing the rhythm of my pulse.

Something inside me stirs.

A whisper—urgent, reckless, undeniable.
Do it.

I have silenced that voice before, buried it beneath logic and hesitation. Tonight, it refuses to stay quiet. It rises, clawing its way back to the surface. My breath fogs the glass, blurring the lights below until the city dissolves into a sea of fire. It feels like a sign.

I know the moment I move, the axis of my world will shift. Nothing will return to what it was. My chest tightens—fear colliding with thrill, resistance giving way to inevitability.

The unknown waits just beyond the glass, calling my name.

So, I draw in a breath.
I steady my heartbeat.
And I step forward.

Into the dark.

Into everything.

This is where my story begins.

Chapter 1
Tehran Beginnings

The world tilted the moment I stepped forward—and when it settled again, it was here, in Tehran. The restless heart of Iran. A city where past and future collide with every breath. I was born into its rhythm: the clang of shopkeepers' shutters at dawn, the scent of rain on dust, the murmured echoes of revolutions long foretold.

My story began here, in a city that never truly sleeps, and in a family whose name carried both honor and expectation.

I was the first grandchild on both sides of my family, a small spark in a lineage already heavy with history and responsibility. The air around those stories always felt thick—like cardamom tea brewing in a crowded kitchen, rich with laughter and secrets passed down through generations.

My father grew up in a home where laughter and arguments shared the same space, where raised voices softened into warmth, and the clinking of dishes marked a strange but familiar harmony.

My mother's world was quieter, more structured, and firmly ruled by tradition—until the two worlds collided. When they did, it felt like opposing seasons meeting: her calm like winter snow against my father's restless spring wind. Uncles, aunts, and grandparents filled every corner of the city, their homes scented with familiar spices and alive with the constant hum of family chatter that never seemed to fade.

During the Shah's era, both of my grandparents were still alive, anchoring our family in pride and tradition. Those years carried a particular fragrance—a blend of jasmine from courtyard gardens and the faint scent of kerosene lamps flickering in quiet hallways at dusk.

My paternal grandfather was a man of rare vision, an entrepreneur far ahead of his time. He owned one of Iran's first General Motors dealerships and operated a successful home-goods store, where the hum of radios mingled with the metallic scent of newly unpacked merchandise. His name was spoken with admiration at gatherings. He embodied progress and prosperity.

Life then felt almost magical—as if even the dust rising from Tehran's old streets shimmered with promise. And yet, beneath it all, the winds of change were already stirring, waiting for their moment.

My maternal grandfather was a true *khan*, a man whose presence symbolized loyalty and prestige. He governed a vast estate near the capital, where sunlight rippled across wheat fields and the scent of freshly turned soil filled the air. His land was alive with sound— hooves striking cobblestones, distant laughter from workers, the rustle of silk dresses in the afternoon breeze.

Farmers and families worked under his protection while maids moved quietly through grand halls, their footsteps echoing against cool marble floors.

Everything changed when the Shah launched the White Revolution—a sweeping effort to redistribute land and wealth. The atmosphere shifted almost overnight, tension settling over the city like a low, unrelenting hum. My grandfather's power dissolved, his wealth reduced to fragments of what it once was. The authority that had defined him faded into silence, replaced by long pauses and the soft rustle of government paperwork.

Faced with this new reality, he made the painful decision to leave his beloved estate and move to Tehran to be closer to family. The journey carried the weight of an ending—the scent of dust and jasmine lingering as the gates closed for the final time, the creak of carriage wheels marking the collapse of an era.

Once a khan with a kingdom to protect, he now carried a quiet vulnerability. I would later recognize it in the way his hands lingered over old photographs, or how his gaze drifted toward the horizon as if searching for something already gone. In rare moments, the grandeur of his past met the humility of loss, revealing the deeply human cost of change.

My paternal grandfather, by contrast, was legendary in a different way. His generosity was known throughout the community. He provided tirelessly for his wife and seven children, the scent of fresh bread and roasted nuts drifting from their home as proof of his devotion. He bought in bulk, ensured there was always food on the table, and sent extra to those in need.

Grain sacks piled in the courtyard. Delivery boys laughed. Life moved in a steady, generous rhythm.

Though he represented progress, he was also nostalgic, sometimes longing for a world that no longer existed. In the evenings, he would sit in his favorite chair, fingers tapping lightly against a teacup, eyes distant with memory. My grandmother grounded him—balancing his generosity with practicality. The soft clink of her bangles and the steadiness of her voice anchored the household.

Together, they formed the heartbeat of the home—strong, familiar, endlessly giving.

I often imagined my grandfather saying quietly, *The world is changing faster than we can keep up. I wonder what the future holds for us.*

And I could see my grandmother smile, her hands resting in her lap, the soft chime of gold punctuating her reply.

We didn't know then that everything we understood was about to be reshaped.

The air between them carried unspoken memories—the scent of tea leaves and rosewater, the faint hum of a distant radio filling the silence. When I was old enough to understand, I realized their love had cost them everything: safety, comfort, reputation. It was not the kind of love celebrated in songs. It was built on quiet defiance, sacrifice, and unwavering loyalty.

Perhaps that was why, even as a child, I mistook defiance for romance.

The spark in my grandmother's eyes, the pride in my grandfather's posture—together, they made rebellion feel like devotion.

As my grandparents adapted to a changing world, Tehran itself pulsed with life. Street vendors roasted nuts. Old taxis belched exhaust. The distant call to prayer rose between apartment buildings. Our family's stories wove themselves into the city's fabric—threads in a tapestry still being formed.

Beneath it all, subtle winds of change whispered of journeys yet to come.

I didn't know it then, but the roots of who I was were already taking hold. The city's hum became the rhythm of my childhood, and somewhere within it, destiny was quietly preparing its stage.

Chapter 2
A House Full of Life

The city roared just beyond our walls, but inside our home, a different kind of life pulsed—loud, layered, electric. On the ground floor, the shop was always awake. Voices overlapped and collided, coins clinked sharply against the counter, and the air carried a heady mix of spices, dust, leather, and fabric drifting in through the open doorway. The city's hum seeped inside, blending with laughter and the steady creak of wooden stairs that connected one world to another.

Above the shop, the bedrooms whispered of dreams still forming. Curtains fluttered in the evening breeze, carrying secrets of childhood hopes and half-imagined futures. And then there was the rooftop—wide, sun-bleached, and open to the sky—daring us to climb higher, see farther, and imagine more.

This was a house where chaos met comfort, where every corner held a story and every step invited adventure. My grandparents' memories lived in the walls. My parents' ambitions shaped the floors beneath our feet. And I—small but alert—began to sense that I was part of something larger than myself.

Even then, as the sun dipped low and painted the city gold, a quiet current of change moved through the house. Invisible. Undeniable. The world beyond our doors was shifting, and soon it would find its way inside. But for now, the adventure had only just begun.

The building itself felt majestic—three and a half stories of constant motion. The moment you stepped in from the busy street, the atmosphere changed. The ground floor buzzed with energy: wrapping paper rustled, voices rose and fell, and the cash register rang out like punctuation in an ongoing conversation.

I can still hear my grandfather's deep, playful voice calling from behind the counter, teasing a customer over the price of a brass lamp. Outside, a vendor roasted nuts, the scent drifting through the open doorway and mingling with leather, fabric, and warm dust— the smell of our family's heartbeat.

Behind the shop, my mother rented a small storage room from my grandfather, adding another layer of family business to an already crowded space.

The second floor offered a brief exhale. A cozy bedroom with its own bathroom served as a quiet retreat, where street noise softened into a distant murmur. It felt suspended between worlds—neither fully public nor fully private.

The third floor was the true heart of the home. Three large bedrooms opened into a sunlit kitchen, a welcoming living room, and a dining area where the scent of saffron and rice lingered long after meals were finished. This was where laughter gathered, where stories spilled across the table between bites, where life felt full, loud, and endlessly shared.

Above it all was the rooftop—fenced, open, and irresistibly inviting. A small kitchen sat tucked into one corner, equipped just enough for late-night snacks beneath the stars. The breeze carried the city's evening rhythm, rooftops stretching endlessly in every direction. A narrow metal ladder led to a tiny upper roof above the kitchen—a secret perch that promised both thrill and danger.

My grandparents occupied the second floor, while the rest of the family filled the third with warmth, chatter, and constant motion. In the middle of a busy neighborhood, my grandfather's shop became a gathering place—lively in the front, quieter in the back—holding both commerce and comfort in equal measure.

My father worked alongside his own father in a nearby store, immersed in the rhythm of business. My mother, a gifted tailor, ran her craft with precision and passion. Her nimble fingers shaped fabric into intricate designs, and each day she taught nearly fifty students, passing down skill, discipline, and quiet confidence.

They met when they were just seventeen.

My mother—fiercely independent and intensely focused on her work—barely noticed my father at first. She was surrounded by bankers and businessmen, yet remained anchored in her craft, balancing ambition with expectation. My father, on the other hand, was captivated from the beginning. He knew she was out of his league, and that knowledge both fueled his determination and revealed his vulnerability.

Their friendship began over shared lunches—simple moments filled with laughter and whispered dreams. Over a year and a half, that friendship deepened into something undeniable. But their love faced resistance. Their families came from different worlds, guided by different values.

Undeterred, they chose to elope.

For six months, they lived in secrecy—moving between temporary hiding places, navigating daily challenges that tested their resolve. Eventually, my maternal grandfather gave his blessing. They married soon after, and not long later, I was born—a symbol of hope, love, and the quiet triumph of defiance.

I arrived in a household already bursting with life. I was adored— by parents, grandparents, uncles, and aunts alike—treated like a little princess from the very beginning. When I was two, my brother Sam was born, adding even more laughter to our crowded home.

But my mother's family was deeply religious, and to them, Tehran felt too liberal—too fast, too exposed. They decided to move to Mashhad, a city known for its conservatism and devotion.

It was a dramatic shift.
And the beginning of another chapter.

Some of my earliest memories come from those years. I remember being three, laughing uncontrollably with my youngest uncle, only five years older than me. Armed with a towel and a spray of water, we soaked the street-facing windows, giggling as passersby glanced up in confusion.

Our backyard offered little privacy, hemmed in by tall buildings, which made the rooftop our sanctuary—our dining room, our gathering place, and sometimes even our bedroom beneath the stars.

One afternoon, curiosity carried me too far. I convinced my uncle to climb onto the tiny roof above the kitchen. I was three. He was eight. From that height, the world spun beneath us—rooftops and streets blurring together.

Fear seized us. We froze.

It was my mother who came looking for us, pulling us back to safety just in time. Without her, the story might have ended very differently.

As the sun set behind Tehran's rooftops, the city's heartbeat continued—steady, insistent. Inside our home, laughter spilled through open windows, mingling with the scent of bread and spices. On the rooftop, shadows stretched long, hiding corners where small adventures waited—unseen, but ready.

Beyond our walls, however, something else was stirring. The streets whispered with unrest, tension slipping into the air in ways no child could fully understand.

Change was coming—sudden, relentless, unstoppable.

Our childhood adventures were far from over.
But the shadows of a new world were already stretching across rooftops and alleys, and nothing would ever feel the same again.

Chapter 3
Shadows of Revolution

I had just curled onto my small mattress, the red blanket my mother had chosen wrapped tightly around me like a promise of safety, when the world fractured.

Screams tore through the quiet of my kindergarten classroom—sharp, sudden, shattering everything I understood. My heart raced. My breath caught. Flames licked at the edges of my vision, curling toward the painted ceiling. Smoke burned my nostrils, thick and suffocating.

For a moment, I froze—small, silent, unable to move in a place that no longer felt safe.

Then strong arms lifted me, carrying me through chaos I could not yet comprehend. The laughter and chatter that once filled my days vanished. So did the familiar scent of my mother's cooking, the steady hum of the city outside. In their place came fire, fear, and confusion.

It was an unexpected beginning—one that would quietly shape everything that followed.

Outside, Tehran's streets appeared unchanged—busy, alive, moving forward as if nothing had happened. But beneath the surface, unrest was spreading, seeping into every home, every family. The revolution was coming. And even without understanding it, I felt its shadow settle over my life.

At five years old, the world suddenly felt vast and unpredictable. The comfort of routine—family gatherings, rooftop adventures, warm kitchens—now carried an edge of urgency. Though I did not yet have words for it, I sensed it clearly: innocence had shifted, and nothing would ever return to the way it had been.

The streets continued their rhythm. Children laughed. Shopkeepers shouted prices across narrow sidewalks. Life pressed on.

But inside me, something had cracked.

Safety felt fragile.
The shadows were no longer distant.

The revolution had begun—quiet, inevitable, unstoppable. And our family, like so many others, would have to adjust, endure, and survive.

I was five when the Shah was ousted, and Khomeini rose to power. My brother was two. My sister was still a newborn. Overnight, the world rearranged itself.

My grandfather lost everything he had built.

My father had no choice but to adapt. He became an eighteen-wheeler truck driver, hauling goods across the country—long, exhausting journeys that kept him away for weeks, sometimes months at a time. The work was grueling, but it allowed my parents to buy a home of their own and begin rebuilding stability from the ground up.

I remember one evening before my father left for another trip. My mother stood at the kitchen counter, packing his lunch with deliberate care. Her movements were slow and tired, but her eyes held both pride and worry.

My father noticed. He placed a gentle hand on her shoulder and smiled.

"We'll get through this," he said. "Together."

In that moment, the weight in the room softened—if only briefly.

Despite everything, tenderness still found its way into our lives. On rare days when my father was home, we gathered in the living room, sharing laughter and simple stories. It was in those quiet pockets of normalcy that I saw how deeply my parents' bond had strengthened under pressure.

Resilience lived in their togetherness.

When I was nearly six, my parents decided to enroll me in school early. At the time, children born in the first half of the year could start ahead of schedule. Family members objected, worried I would struggle later—that I was too young.

16

But my parents trusted their instincts.
And they trusted me.

School was not effortless. Math challenged me in particular. Three plus eight should have been eleven, but I insisted it was twelve. After second grade, my mother homeschooled me through the summer, determined to help me catch up.

On exam day, she stood just outside the classroom door, hoping her presence would anchor me.

Still, I answered eight plus three as twelve.

Those small mistakes fueled concern that starting early might hold me back.

But life had already begun teaching me perseverance.

By nine, my parents trusted me with real responsibility. One morning, they handed me a large pot and a hundred toman and sent me to fetch breakfast—Persian *halim*, thick and comforting, made from wheat and turkey.

The walk took twenty minutes. The air smelled of dust and fresh bread as shopkeepers set up for the day. The vendor filled the pot until it overflowed, and I could barely lift it.

Every few steps, I had to stop and rest. My arms burned. The street felt endless.

But I kept going.

When I finally reached home—soaked in sweat and triumphant—my uncle laughed and said, "We didn't actually need that much."

I stared at him, exhausted.

Then I burst out laughing.

I had done it.

That morning, I wasn't just a child running an errand. I was victorious.

The revolution touched everyone.

One afternoon, I overheard our elderly neighbor, Mrs. Azimi, speaking with Mr. Rahimi down the street.

"Prices are rising again," she said quietly.

"Yes," he replied, scanning the road as if trouble might appear at any moment. "Even the children feel it."

Her small garden smelled faintly of jasmine as she sighed. "I just hope we find peace."

The fires faded.
The smoke cleared.

But nothing was the same.

The shadows had arrived—
and they were here to stay.

Chapter 4
First Lessons in Responsibility

We reached the new house just as the sun slipped behind the horizon. Dust hovered in the air, glowing briefly in the fading light. The walls were unfinished—pale, bare—as if the house itself were waiting to be claimed.

Inside, every step echoed. The rooms stretched outward—wide, open, unfamiliar. The kitchen gleamed. The bedrooms rose upward. And the rooftop beckoned with both promise and risk. My siblings scattered immediately, their laughter bright but small against the vastness of the space.

I felt it the moment we walked in: this house needed more than furniture and footsteps.
It needed order.
It needed care.

And somehow, at ten years old, I understood that part of that responsibility now belonged to me.

The neighborhood was new, still under construction—twenty houses planned, only two completed. It felt exposed, unfinished, too open. People could come and go easily. As you entered through the massive metal gates, there was enough space to drive two cars side by side into the yard. To the right, two long gardens stretched toward the house, their soil untouched, waiting for roots to take hold.

Beneath the building was covered parking for several cars and a small storage room. A staircase led up into the main living area. The kitchen was enormous, opening into a dining room on one side and a spacious living room straight ahead. To the left were four large bedrooms, each with oversized windows that opened onto a shared balcony. Every room had its own bathroom—a luxury we had never known before.

My parents had their room.
I had mine.
My brother and sister had theirs.

It was a beautiful home.
But beauty did not quiet my unease.

My brother Sam, two years younger than me, moved through the house quietly. He wore oversized glasses that slipped down his nose, earning him endless teasing—mostly from me. We joked that if he held them toward the sun, he could start a fire. He pretended to be annoyed, but his kindness was unmistakable. Sam noticed things others missed. He carried a gentle patience, a quiet intelligence that revealed itself in moments of stillness.

One afternoon, when I was ready to brush away a line of ants in the garden, Sam crouched beside them.
"Let's watch," he said softly.

He found wonder in the smallest details, reminding me—without trying—to slow down.

My sister May, five years younger than me, was the opposite of chaos. She listened. She followed rules. She excelled effortlessly. Where I tested boundaries, May embodied calm. She had a natural grace that settled rooms. I remember her kneeling beside a younger child at the park, comforting them after a fall—her touch instinctive and steady.

She taught me that strength could be quiet.

Then there was Ray, the youngest—just two years old. Sweet. Curious. Endlessly charming. He toddled through the house like a spark of light, his laughter softening every edge. I became his shadow, his babysitter, his protector. Even at that age, he had a way of making people feel seen, special, and needed.

One night, when I was ten, fear arrived uninvited.

My father was away on another long trip, and the house felt too large without him. The night was unnaturally still when my mother froze mid-step. Footsteps crunched softly on the gravel below.

She moved toward the stairwell and peered into the darkness. A shadow shifted—unfamiliar, wrong.

In that instant, she chose courage.

"Oh, you're finally here!" she called out, her voice steady. "Come on up—everyone's waiting!"

Her hand trembled.
Her voice did not.

The shadow hesitated—then disappeared into the night.

That was the first time I saw fear and bravery share the same breath.

Months later, I faced my own version of that moment.

My parents had stepped out, leaving me with my siblings and cousins—eight children in total. After dinner, I heard footsteps below. A shadow lingered near the parking area.

I remembered my mother.

"Uncle!" I called, forcing calm into my voice. "Come on up— we're waiting!"

The shadow paused.
Then vanished.

I locked the door, gathered the children, and spread blankets across the living-room floor.
"We're having a sleepover," I said lightly.
They laughed.

I stayed awake long after they slept—listening, protecting, hoping.

That night, responsibility settled into me like a second skin.

Beyond our walls, Tehran was changing rapidly. The city's rhythm sharpened. Rumors traveled faster. Safety felt temporary.

Inside our home, I learned my first real lesson:

Courage is not loud.
Leadership does not wait for permission.

The challenges had begun.
And the girl I was becoming had already started to stand watch.

Chapter 5
Childhood Joy and War

The sky over Tehran never felt the same again.

By the time I was ten, I understood that the night could hold both stars and bombs.

Every evening, the sirens wailed at eight sharp—metallic, piercing, impossible to ignore. The lights went out. Windows darkened. Streets emptied. Above us, planes moved like predators, circling, searching, claiming the sky as their own. It was the beginning of the Iran–Iraq War, though at the time we could not yet grasp how long its shadow would stretch across our lives.

My mother held my hand tightly as she guided us to our nightly refuge—an unfinished space of dirt and concrete, cranes and half-built walls rising around us like silent giants. The ground felt cold beneath my feet. The air vibrated with fear. Hearts pounded. Shadows shifted.

Each night was an endurance test.

Each morning, a fragile victory.

And yet, even there, something stubborn survived.

A quiet spark of courage—unspoken but unyielding—whispered the same message every night: *endure*. Life would go on. Somehow, even here, joy would find a way.

The war was never far away.

One night, barely a mile and a half from our home, a massive park erupted into flame. The sky burned orange. The ground shook beneath us. Fear stopped being abstract—it became physical, alive, something that pressed against our chests and refused to leave.

After the sirens faded, I often lay awake, staring at the ceiling, wondering how the same sky could cradle both stars and destruction. In the mornings, life resumed with quiet defiance. My mother brewed tea. Bread toasted. The scent of normalcy filled the air, as if the night before had never happened.

That was how we survived—by insisting on ordinary moments.

There was a rhythm to those years. No matter how the day unfolded—school, laughter, play—we all felt the shift as evening approached. At eight, the sirens returned. The bombings followed. Night after night—month after month.

Still, my parents remained calm. They made us feel protected, teaching us—without words—that fear did not get to decide how we lived.

Responsibility came early.

My mother taught me everything in the kitchen, shaping me into someone who could cook for gatherings of twenty or more. My sister May became my steady helper—quiet, reliable. When my father returned from long trips, my parents disappeared into each other's presence, and it fell to us to restore order to the house. We divided the chores—cleaning, laundry, flowers, bathrooms—and finished everything before they walked through the door.

It wasn't a burden.
It was our contribution.

Every summer, we escaped Tehran and drove to my mother's hometown, Mashhad. The shift was immediate—as if we had stepped out of a battlefield and into a sanctuary. Prayer calls replaced sirens. Fear softened into routine.

My grandparents' house stood near a mosque, its call to prayer echoing through the walls five times a day. They oversaw mosque programs, organized meals for the homeless, and made sure no one in the neighborhood went without food. The house was always alive—neighbors arriving with trays, voices filling the courtyard, the air thick with the scent of stews and fresh bread.

Because my grandparents were deeply traditional, we prepared ourselves carefully before arriving—scarves adjusted, coats buttoned, roles resumed. Inside, the rhythm of faith and family took over.

My favorite place was the basement.

A low wooden table sat beneath a thick quilt, a small gas heater glowing underneath. We tucked our feet beneath the blanket as warmth crept upward. Tea steamed. Cardamom scented the air. One by one, uncles, aunts, and cousins arrived until nearly twenty of us crowded around the table—laughing, eating, alive.

We always visited the Haram, the Imam's shrine.

I didn't yet fully understand faith, but inside those marble walls—surrounded by bowed heads and whispered prayers—I felt something deeper than fear.

Calm.
Possibility.

I pressed my hands against the cool stone and whispered prayers for forgiveness, gratitude, and peace.

Those summers felt like another world—slower, softer, anchored in belief and belonging. They reminded me that even in the middle of war, life could still be sacred.

When we returned to Tehran, the sirens awaited us.

Childhood slipped through my fingers one night at a time. But courage stayed. It flickered in small acts—helping, cooking, laughing, praying. I didn't yet know what storms lay ahead or how deeply the war would shape me.

I only knew this:

Joy and fear had learned to live side by side.

And somewhere beyond the horizon, the next chapter was already forming.

Chapter 6
Adventures, Discipline, and Play

The ball skidded across cracked asphalt, slamming into the wall with a sharp thud. I sprinted after it, sneakers slapping the dusty street, my hair whipping against sunburned cheeks.

"You're too slow!" I shouted, laughing, as my brothers groaned in protest.

This was my world—scraped knees, sun-warmed skin, and games without rules. My mother's voice floated from the house, reminding me to be careful, to act like a proper girl. I barely listened. Out there, beneath the relentless sun, I was fast, fearless, and entirely myself.

Somewhere between the laughter and the falls, I felt it—the thrill of movement, of freedom, of possibility. Something stirred inside me, a quiet certainty that life beyond these streets was waiting, vast and unpredictable.

My mother tried to shape me into her vision of the ideal girl— skilled in the kitchen, attentive to the home, graceful in movement. I learned all of it. But alongside that discipline, I was already sketching another version of myself: messy, sun-tanned, and fueled by dreams that refused to fit neatly into expectation.

Back then, girls didn't play soccer.

I did anyway.

Every day, I slipped outside with my brothers and their friends, hat pulled low, ponytail tied tight. I came home bruised and scraped, skin darkened by the sun, smiling without apology. My mother would shake her head.

"You're a girl," she'd say. "You should look more ladylike."

I nodded—and ran right back out.

My love for soccer eventually convinced my father to do something bold. Despite the strict rules barring women from stadiums, he took me to a match. He tied my hair back, tucked it beneath a cap, dressed me in loose clothes, and erased every visible sign of who I was. With my brother, my uncle, and my cousins, we blended into the crowd.

Sitting in the front row, the stadium roared around me—dust, sweat, shouts, thunderous cheers. Men cursed freely. My uncle watched me in disbelief. My father only smiled.

"She's fine," he said. "She can handle it."

I clutched his arm, heart racing, exhilarated and terrified at once. It felt like we were carrying a secret too big for words. That day stayed with me—a reminder that courage sometimes looks like bending rules quietly, just enough to let a child breathe.

Persian New Year—Nowruz—was another kind of joy.

My mother sewed matching dresses for my sister and me, crisp shirts for my brothers. We gathered around the Haft-Seen table, watching goldfish dart through their bowl, waiting for the exact moment spring arrived. Gifts were unwrapped. Laughter filled the room. Soon, the house overflowed with relatives, plates heavy with food, voices rising in celebration. In those moments, it was impossible not to feel rich.

Travel was another gift my father gave us. His eighteen-wheeler became our gateway to the country. Every holiday, we packed up and joined him on deliveries—Shiraz, Isfahan, Bandar Abbas, Kerman. My mother prepared food for days. The truck's cab became our moving home, its two-level bed holding all of us like a secret refuge.

At rest stops, my parents grilled kebabs beside the road. Smoke curled into the open sky. Music hummed softly as the engine cooled. I fell asleep to the rhythm of the highway, rocked by motion and safety.

My father also traveled to Europe for work, returning with clothes, shoes, and gifts we couldn't find at home. He kept his earnings tucked away carefully, and when my parents were gone, I was entrusted with quiet responsibility—maintaining the house, locking doors, setting the table perfectly before their return. Discipline shaped our days, but we never lacked.

Some of my happiest memories came from the sea.

My father rented beachside villas where cousins, uncles, and siblings gathered in joyful chaos. One afternoon, he loaded us onto a giant inner tube and pushed us into deeper water, flipping it without warning. Panic and laughter collided as we surfaced sputtering. I was the oldest and barely knew how to swim, but he watched closely, making sure no one drifted too far. Fear taught us quickly. Laughter followed.

One night, unable to sleep, I slipped out to the beach alone. The ocean was dark, the moon hidden, the waves barely visible. To my surprise, my uncles and aunts were already there, laughing quietly. They invited me into the water. At eleven years old, I stepped into the sea after midnight, heart pounding, exhilaration overpowering fear. It felt like a rite of passage—silent, wild, unforgettable.

Another summer, a familiar figure appeared on the shoreline—a barefoot man with a worn bag slung across his back, calling out in fluent Farsi, "Snacks! I've got snacks!"

He was Russian, but Iran had become his home.

That evening, he asked to speak with our parents. After watching us play, he turned to me.

"I'm a fortune teller," he said. "Do you want to know your future?"

He took my hands, studying them carefully.

"You will go far," he said at last. "You won't stay here. You will have children. You will be successful."

I laughed, running back to my siblings, shouting that I would leave and they would stay. That night, the villa buzzed with laughter, food, and possibility. I didn't know then how accurate his words would be—but something inside me believed them.

Dance was another language my mother insisted I learn.

Though she herself moved gently, she filled the house with music. My father brought home VHS tapes from Europe—ballet, modern dance, breakdancing. I studied every movement, practicing tirelessly.

After dinner, I became the family's performer. Traditional Persian dances gave way to playful improvisation. Sometimes I pulled my sister into the rhythm. At gatherings, everyone watched, clapping and laughing, while the room filled with motion and sound. Even now, when I hear those melodies, my body remembers before my mind does.

Those years were filled with motion—across streets, highways, water, and dance floors. Childhood unfolded between discipline and freedom, fear and joy. I didn't yet know how quickly things would change, or how much strength life would demand of me.

But somewhere deep inside, I felt it:

I was being prepared.

34

And the next chapter was already waiting.

Chapter 7
School Life and Rebellion

Middle school arrived like a sudden storm. The hallways smelled of chalk dust and sweat, and the air buzzed with whispers, glances, and rules that shifted depending on who was watching. At home, expectations were clear and unwavering—chores, discipline, excellence. At school, the boundaries felt invisible, tempting, alive.

I learned quickly how to live between worlds.

I wore obedience like a uniform, but beneath it, something restless took shape. Rebellion didn't always announce itself loudly. Sometimes it was a hidden smile, a borrowed book, a laugh swallowed at the wrong moment. Each small act carried electricity—the first taste of independence.

My mother's standards never softened. By twelve, I could run a kitchen on my own, standing on a stool to see into oversized pots, stirring with determination. After chores, she played music and asked my sister and me to dance, turning discipline into performance. She pushed me forward relentlessly. That drive carried into academics as well. Even though I had started school early, she homeschooled me through the summer before middle school. By twelve, I had passed the seventh-grade exam and entered eighth grade, putting me on track to graduate high school at sixteen.

Outside our home, the country tightened.

Movies were censored. Television showed only what was approved—no romance, no touch, hair always covered. But my father had a quiet connection. Every Thursday night, a friend arrived with a stack of VHS tapes smuggled in from abroad. From Thursday evening through Friday night, our living room transformed into a secret theater.

We watched *Rocky*, Clint Eastwood westerns, and stories that felt forbidden and thrilling. We laughed softly, always alert, knowing discovery could mean fines—or worse. Those nights taught me something important: freedom sometimes lived in shadows.

My parents balanced each other perfectly. My mother-built structure; my father invited risk.

When I was thirteen, he returned from a trip and took me for a drive in his Camaro. On an empty stretch of road, he pulled over and handed me the keys.

"Your turn."

My heart raced. I had never driven—never even touched a manual transmission. My knees shook as he calmly guided me through the gears. Fear gave way to exhilaration. Trust settled between us like a promise. My father made courage feel possible.

Among my siblings, I was the mischievous one—but my heart always led. One Mother's Day, I secretly collected everyone's allowance and walked thirty minutes to a clothing store after school. I chose a shirt and a scarf I knew my mother would love. By the time I returned home, panic filled the house. There were no phones. No way to find me.

When I walked through the door and revealed the gift, worry melted into laughter. My mother's smile was worth every step.

Outside, rules hardened.

Guards patrolled the streets. Schools were segregated. Makeup—even a trace—meant punishment. One morning, a guard pressed a cotton pad to my eyelid, revealing faint residue from the night before. The cotton was taped into my report card. My behavior grade dropped to a B.

I couldn't help laughing at the absurdity.

Difference, I learned early, carried consequences.

That incident pushed my parents to search for alternatives. They found a Christian school in Tehran—one of the first of its kind. I became the first Muslim student enrolled there. It changed everything.

Morning prayers were shared—seven minutes for Christians, seven for Muslims. After months of listening, I knew both by heart. One morning, when the Christian student assigned to lead prayer was absent, the principal asked for a volunteer.

My hand rose without hesitation.

Standing before 150 students, I delivered the prayer flawlessly. Later, my counselor gently warned me that I shouldn't do it again. I smiled. Faith, to me, felt bigger than divisions.

Friendship flourished there. Laughter grew louder. Stories bolder. Curiosity encouraged. I began visiting church with friends, stepping into spaces that felt both foreign and familiar. Sunlight filtered through stained glass, casting color across wooden pews. Candles scented the air. I felt calm—not converted, not conflicted—just open.

Eventually, friends visited my home. They were surprised.

"Your life is just like ours," they said.

They were right.

Our home existed apart from the tension outside. Music played. Alcohol appeared at gatherings. Hijabs stayed off indoors. Politics remained outside the door. My parents taught us another form of discipline—the control of words. No profanity. No shouting. Disagreements lived quietly.

I never heard my parents fight. Instead, silence spoke. Tea was poured twice—once for us, once for my father. A question asked indirectly carried meaning without confrontation. Love lived in restraint.

Those years shaped me profoundly. Between rules and rebellion, faith and freedom, fear and laughter, I learned how to stand in contradiction without breaking. The world outside tightened its grip, but inside me, something expanded.

I didn't yet know how much would change—or how quickly childhood would disappear.

I only knew this:

I was learning to choose my own voice.

Chapter 8
Teenage Milestones

By tenth grade, life felt like a careful dance between shadows and scrutiny. Rules pressed in from every direction, and one wrong step could ripple far beyond detention or a reprimand. Authority watched closely, but temptation lingered everywhere, and the thrill of pushing against boundaries stirred something restless inside me.

That was when I met Lily.

She was chaos wrapped in confidence—reckless, magnetic, unapologetic. Lily lived as if rules were suggestions meant for other people. Her grades were poor, her reputation worse, and teachers had long since stopped trying to rein her in. Her father had been a *shahid*, a martyr of the war, and she lived alone with her mother and younger brother. Their home was warm but unstructured, and Lily wore that freedom like armor.

My mother warned me immediately.
"Stay away from her," she said. "She's trouble."

Maybe she was. But something about Lily pulled at me. She moved through the world without hesitation, fearless in ways I had never allowed myself to be. Where I paused, she leapt.

One morning, she leaned toward me in class, her eyes sparkling.
"Let's skip school."

My stomach tightened. I shook my head, but she smiled as if she already knew the answer. At recess, she led me behind the school to a hidden corner where a metal barrel rested against the wall. Without hesitation, she climbed up and swung herself over.

My heart pounded as I followed—every movement a betrayal of everything I had been taught.

We landed on the other side laughing, breathless, and giddy. Almost immediately, Lily flagged down a passing car—a sleek silver Mercedes that slowed and stopped beside us. She slid into the front seat like it was the most natural thing in the world. I climbed into the back, suspended between disbelief and fear.

The driver was young and handsome. Lily spoke to him easily, confidently, as if they were old friends. He took us to a quiet restaurant tucked away from watchful eyes. White tablecloths. Polished silverware. The illusion of adulthood. It all felt unreal.

At one point, Lily opened the glove compartment and pulled out a small camera.
"What's this?" she asked casually.
"My camera," he replied.
"It's nice," she said, turning it in her hands.
"You can have it."

She accepted it without surprise.

That was Lily. She didn't ask permission. She simply took what was offered.

After lunch, they exchanged numbers. As we stepped out of the car, my chest buzzed with adrenaline and guilt.
"You're really going to call him?" I whispered.
She laughed. "Of course not. He's just part of the story."

I didn't yet understand how quickly stories could turn.

Growing up in a country shaped by revolution and war meant constant restraint. Guards patrolled the streets. Social rules tightened. Public affection was forbidden. Schools were segregated. Hijabs were mandatory. Makeup was policed. Female guards inspected us daily, searching for violations—in our bags, on our faces, even in the way we stood.

Inside our home, life followed a different rhythm. Music played. Laughter flowed. My father's time in Europe shaped his worldview, and our family lived slightly outside the mainstream. We weren't political. We weren't loud. We simply refused to let fear define us.

One afternoon, I went out for coffee with my uncle—my mother's brother—who was visiting from another city. It should have been simple. Instead, a National Guard patrol stopped us, blocking our path.

IDs were demanded. Questions followed.

Why didn't our last names match?

How were we related?

They didn't believe us.

We were taken in for questioning, the ordinary afternoon twisting into something cold and frightening. The walls felt too close. Time stretched thin. Eventually, my parents arrived—calm, firm, undeniable. They explained. They vouched. We were released.

Relief washed over me. But the lesson remained.

In this world, innocence was not protection.

Despite everything, my parents kept politics out of our home. Stability mattered more than opinion. We were anchored in deliberate kindness—shared meals, respect, restraint.

Sometimes, even clothing became a target. My father once brought my brother sneakers from Europe. At school, he was bullied and attacked for wearing them. Later, a banana from Turkey caused the same reaction.

Difference, I learned, could be dangerous.

The private Christian high school became one of the most transformative choices of my life. Friendship felt freer there. Humor flowed. Curiosity was welcomed. We shared sleepovers, conversations, secrets. Religion was not a battlefield—it was a background thread.

We believed in God. But we believed in one another, too.

At fourteen, I stood before a room full of students and spoke prayers that were not my own—and felt no conflict doing so. Faith, to me, was connection, not division.

When my father returned from trips, he asked for reports—grades, behavior. If he approved, he handed me money.
"Do whatever you want with it."

I never spent it on myself. I took my siblings and cousins to the movies, then out for sandwiches. Paying for everyone filled me with a quiet joy I didn't yet have words for.

Even then, I felt it—the pull toward something beyond these streets, these rules, these years.

Adolescence wasn't just rebellion.
It was awakening.

Childhood was slipping away.
And something far more complicated was waiting.

I was already stepping toward it.

Chapter 9
Adolescence and Family Dynamics

Skipping school became my secret thrill—an adrenaline rush that made every day feel like an adventure. By tenth grade, that recklessness finally caught up with me.

I failed my English class.

My parents had no idea. They had already planned a summer trip to Yugoslavia with my siblings. I was left behind—supposedly to study for my redo exam—under my aunt's watchful eye.

Studying, of course, was optional in my world.

My aunt was playful and carefree, more accomplice than authority. Instead of textbooks, I spent my days racing through the streets, kicking a soccer ball with neighborhood boys, laughing until my sides hurt, completely forgetting the exam looming ahead like a ticking time bomb.

The day of reckoning arrived.

My aunt, ever the enabler, announced cheerfully, "Let's have a good lunch before your exam!"

We wandered to a nearby restaurant, ate, laughed, and lingered—far too long. When we finally walked into the school, it was 1:15 p.m., two hours past the scheduled 11:00 exam.

The halls were eerily quiet. Only a few teachers and the principal remained.

My heart pounded as I approached her, forcing my voice to sound casual.
"I'm here for my redo exam."

She looked at me, unimpressed.
"You're two hours late," she said. "You've missed it."

The words hit like a freight train.

Panic surged. Disbelief followed close behind. My parents were due back in a week, expecting everything to be perfect. Instead, I had failed again, while my siblings were traveling abroad.

When my father's truck finally pulled into the driveway days later, I ran outside. My skin was bronzed from endless days in the sun. My hair was cut far too short. Guilt and defiance clung to me equally.

My mother gasped.
"What happened to you? Your skin—your hair!"
Then she turned to my aunt. "I can't believe you."

We survived the first day without revealing the exam disaster. But the next morning, the truth surfaced. My aunt confessed. My parents were stunned.

My father stormed to the school, pleading for mercy. The response was cold and final: *maybe*—maybe two weeks before the new school year—*if* enough students needed a redo.

The summer dragged on like a slow-motion thriller—dread, regret, and waiting tangled together. Then, one week before school started, the call came.

Enough students had signed up.

I took the exam.
I passed.

That summer became a blur of mischief, panic, and near-disaster—a chapter I would never forget.

As my sixteenth birthday approached, I decided to invite about fifty friends from school. When I mentioned it casually at dinner, my mother froze.

She asked how I had planned a party without knowing her intentions.

I smiled. "I assumed you'd throw one," I said. "So I took the initiative."

The date? Friday.
Two days away.
Guest count? About seventy-five, including family.

Her eyes nearly popped out of her head.

Despite the chaos, my parents made it unforgettable. The house filled with music, food, and laughter. My father had just bought a brand-new Canon camera from Europe and proudly carried it all night—photographing my dress, the guests, the food, the joy. Or so we thought.

After the party, we went to a photo shop to develop the film. I sat in the back seat beside my mother, still buzzing from the night. My father requested one-hour processing, smiling with anticipation.

When he returned, his shoulders sagged. His eyes stayed on the ground.

"What happened?" my mother asked.

"The camera wasn't turned on," he said quietly. "It clicked—but it didn't take a single picture. Not one."

Her eyes filled with tears.
"That's not fair," she whispered. "We can't redo it. It's gone."

No one spoke.

The silence felt sacred—the kind that follows loss. In that moment, I understood how fragile memories are, how happiness can disappear without leaving proof.

Just as I turned sixteen, my mother laid out her vision for my future with surgical precision. One evening, after my father returned from a trip, we piled into the car for dinner. Streetlights streaked past as we drove by the nursing university and the nearby hospital.

"That's your next destination," she said calmly. "Once you finish high school, you're going to become a nurse."

Her words landed heavily in my chest. This wasn't a suggestion. It was a roadmap.

I stared at the building, feeling both the weight of her certainty and a quiet pull toward the unknown.

Life was changing faster than I could absorb. Familiar sounds—the call to prayer, alleyway chatter, the creak of our front gate—began to feel like quiet goodbyes.

As government restrictions tightened and neighbors grew cautious, life became more complicated. My parents saw what others refused to acknowledge. They had witnessed alternatives in Europe. A safer future existed elsewhere.

The plan began with my younger brother, Sam. If he reached military age, he could be drafted and sent to war. My father arranged for him to escape to Turkey, where friends would help him settle. Meanwhile, my parents sold our home and moved into a smaller apartment, preparing the rest of us to follow.

We packed our lives into boxes—each one heavy with hope and unspoken fear.

That night, sleep wouldn't come. The apartment felt unnaturally quiet. My parents whispered behind closed doors. My brother's suitcase sat half-packed, waiting for a journey I wasn't ready to imagine.

I pressed my forehead against the cool window glass and stared at the city glowing beneath the streetlights.

Change was coming—not the ordinary kind, but the kind that reshapes everything you thought was permanent.

In the stillness, anticipation flickered inside me.

Nothing would ever be the same again.

Chapter 10
Forbidden Love Begins

The new house was silent—almost too quiet—as if it were holding its breath. I had unpacked the last boxes and adjusted the final picture frame, and for a brief moment, the world outside seemed to pause with me.

That was when I sensed it.

A presence—subtle but unmistakable. A gaze that didn't belong to anyone I knew, yet felt as though it was waiting for me to look away.

At sixteen, I thought I already understood excitement, fear, and the thrill of small rebellions. But this was different. It felt electric. Almost forbidden. The house seemed to whisper through its walls, and the shadows stretching along the staircase sent my pulse racing. I couldn't see anything yet, but I knew something was there.

That realization tugged at my curiosity, daring me to step into a world I wasn't ready for—and still, I couldn't resist.

That night, sitting in the sunroom and watching the neighborhood settle beneath the glow of streetlights, a new story quietly began. It was a story shaped by risk, desire, and rules waiting to be broken—a story that would alter everything I believed about love, family, and myself.

Moving into the three-story rental felt like discovering a hidden gem. From the street, a short set of steps led down to the parking area, bordered by a small yard and storage space. A few steps up brought you into the main living level—a careful balance of comfort and elegance. To the right was a spacious kitchen with large windows facing the front, bright and welcoming. Beyond it stretched a vast living area and a grand dining room, made for family gatherings.

Just around the corner stood the sunroom—entirely glass, rising all the way to the roof. It flooded the space with light and offered a quiet retreat. Down the hall were a generous bathroom, a laundry area, and four bedrooms—one for my parents, one for me, and two for my siblings. Another baby was on the way, and the house already felt full of anticipation.

Despite its beauty, something in the air felt different. A stillness lingered, as if the walls themselves were waiting to witness stories not yet told.

While my father was away on one of his long trips—this time visiting my brother Sam in Turkey—the responsibility of moving fell entirely on my mother and me. Though physically absent, my father's presence seemed woven into the house, felt rather than seen. Sam's voice reached us through crackling phone calls and late-night laughter, reminding us how stretched our family had become across borders.

My mother, seven months pregnant, moved through the house with quiet determination. Even surrounded by towering boxes and visible exhaustion, she found order in chaos. She guided me not only with instructions, but with the steady grace of someone who had weathered life's storms and learned to trust her own strength.

She leaned on me more than ever, and suddenly I wasn't just a teenager—I was helping steer our household through transition. Each cleared corner, each lifted box, felt like a small victory. My muscles ached, sweat clung to my skin, yet there was a strange exhilaration in the responsibility.

Childhood had slipped quietly away. One day, you are helping. The next, you are anchoring everyone else.

Just as the last box was set aside, a gentle voice called from the stairway. I looked up and saw her—a kind woman introducing herself as Mrs. Bonlou, the owner's wife. She was in her sixties, with a warmth that felt timeless. She appeared at our door holding a plate of sweets, smiling as if she had known us forever.

Her kindness carried something rare—ease, sincerity, a belief in small gestures. The exhaustion melted from our shoulders as she spoke. Even after she left, the sweetness of her presence lingered, like a promise that this house would hold more than memories.

Perhaps even secrets.

That simple act changed the day. The weight of responsibility eased, replaced by a sense of warmth and belonging. Our moving day became something more than tiring—it became unforgettable.

A few days later, my mother chatted with Mrs. Bonlou and learned more about the family who owned the building. When she told me about them, it felt as if she were introducing characters in a story waiting to unfold—four sons, each walking a different path.

The youngest was twenty, still a student.
The third, Seud, was twenty-two and worked for an air-conditioning company—practical and steady.
Faye, twenty-six, managed his father's tire business, confident and grounded.
The eldest, thirty, was married and lived upstairs, sharing the same floor plan—perhaps listening to the same morning sounds echo through the building.

Their names stayed with me longer than I expected.

As we settled into new routines and I counted down the months to my early high-school graduation, life took on a different rhythm. School was nearby, but my parents preferred a private minibus. My aunt and mother remained inseparable, and soon my uncle and aunt moved just one street away. Family felt closer than ever, woven tightly into daily life.

Still, something inside me was changing.

I became more aware of myself—of how others might see me. Maybe it was the new house. Maybe it was time. In the mirror, I noticed my soft beige complexion, my height—five feet five—and the way my dark curls fell just above my hips. My light-brown eyes carried a spark that drew people in before I spoke. I saw my mother's strength in my posture, my father's quiet resolve in my gaze.

I looked like someone ready for something new, even if I didn't yet know what shape it would take.

Evenings often found me sitting in the sunroom, watching light pour through the glass as the neighborhood came alive. During the quiet before dinner, faint sounds drifted down from above— laughter, footsteps, music, the clatter of tools. I didn't know whose voices they were, but something about them made my heart race.

It wasn't just curiosity.

It was awareness.

Sometimes I glanced upward, pretending to watch the sky, and caught the faint outline of movement behind a curtain—a silhouette. Even shadows can feel like invitations when you are sixteen, and the world suddenly feels too big for your chest.

One evening, my mother asked me to take a tray of sweets upstairs to the landlady. The stairwell smelled of cool air and wood. As I climbed, a door opened softly one floor above—not the one I was headed toward.

I hesitated.

For a brief moment, I felt it again—a gaze. Curious. Gentle. Almost expectant. I didn't see a face, only the warmth of presence, the pause between heartbeats.

Then the door closed.

I continued climbing.

Later that night, the sunroom glass reflected my face—flushed cheeks, bright eyes, a smile I couldn't explain. Something had shifted. I didn't yet know what it meant, but the air carried a new tone—faint, thrilling, like the first note of a melody that would soon become impossible to ignore.

Whatever had begun that night, I knew one thing for sure:

It would not end easily.

Chapter 11
Heart Entwined

The days that followed felt suspended, like holding my breath between two worlds. Morning light streamed through the curtains as if nothing had changed, yet everything inside me had shifted. Each sound—the knock of a door, footsteps on the stairs, the low hum of the refrigerator—felt charged with both possibility and risk.

Love, I was learning, doesn't always arrive with a declaration. Sometimes it slips in quietly, through shared glances, unspoken words, and silences that say more than speech ever could.

The hush between us grew heavier, richer—carrying the weight of something no one dared name. The familiar rhythm of family life—chores, conversations, my mother's watchful presence—blurred into the background. Every accidental crossing of paths wove another invisible thread between us. Secrets have their own tempo: faint at first, then louder, until the heart can no longer pretend not to hear them.

The next morning began like any other. Sunlight spilled across the kitchen counter. My mother hummed softly as she stirred her tea. The scent of fresh bread filled the air. Yet something in me felt altered, as though the world had tilted slightly overnight.

I told myself it was nothing—just the excitement of a new house, new routines. But when I stepped outside to hang laundry in the small yard near the parking area, the hum returned. The air felt sharper. Colors brighter. Footsteps above carried a warmth I hadn't noticed before.

Then I saw him.

He appeared at the top of the stairway—tall, relaxed, unaware of how the light seemed to follow him. His sleeves were rolled halfway up his arms, revealing sun-warmed skin. His dark hair was slightly tousled, shaped more by wind than intention. He carried a small box, shifting its weight as he walked.

When our eyes met, everything else fell away.

It wasn't a stare—just a glance. But in that instant, the world went quiet. His eyes, deep brown threaded with gold, held an easy calm—and beneath it, something unguarded that mirrored my own.

"Good morning," he said, his voice warm and steady.

"Good morning," I replied, softer than I meant to.

He smiled—not wide or practiced, just enough to leave warmth lingering in the space between us—then nodded and disappeared around the corner. But the memory of that smile stayed.

The rest of the day passed in a blur. Laundry folded itself imperfectly. Words on the page refused to settle. I told myself glances meant nothing.

But I already knew they did.

Later that afternoon, my mother mentioned running into one of the Bonlou sons on her way back from the store.

"Such a polite young man," she said casually. "Seud, I think. He works for an air-conditioning company. He offered to help if ours ever breaks. What a lovely family."

I forced indifference. "That's nice."

But his name echoed long after.

That evening, standing in the sunroom as daylight softened into gold, I realized I was listening for footsteps—not deliberately, but instinctively. The world dimmed into shadow, and I smiled without knowing why.

Seud was not a man who sought attention; it followed him naturally. He stood about five-foot-eleven, with broad shoulders and the lean strength of someone accustomed to work, not display. His bronze skin spoke of long hours outdoors. His dark, slightly wavy hair resisted being fully tamed.

His eyes were his most striking feature—deep brown, threaded with gold, quietly knowing. A faint scar rested above his right eyebrow, subtle but unforgettable, hinting at a story he would only tell if asked twice. When he smiled, it softened everything, revealing warmth beneath restraint.

His voice carried the same ease—steady, thoughtful, unhurried. He chose his words carefully, often letting silence speak first. He took pride in his work. His hands told their own story—strong, capable, lightly scarred, yet gentle in motion.

What set him apart was not appearance alone, but presence.

From the very first glance, he didn't simply appear in my life—he arrived.

Days later, we crossed paths again in the stairwell. His greeting was warm, unassuming. A connection flickered—unmistakable. From the kitchen window, I could see the parking lot and street, and soon I found myself noticing arrivals and departures more than I should have.

Sometimes our eyes met from a distance—just a smile, brief and shared. It felt forbidden, and that made it intoxicating.

Our silent ritual became mutual. He often stood at his kitchen window, timing it perfectly. Every morning as I boarded the school bus, I glanced upward, and there he was. In the afternoons, he appeared again, as if by coincidence.

One morning, as I waited for the bus, I heard his voice behind me.

"Hey."

I turned to see him standing a few steps down the stairway, smiling shyly.

"I have something for you."

Glancing around, he added quietly, "No one can see us."

He placed a small bottle of perfume in my hand.

"I thought you might like it."

I thanked him, my heart racing, and slipped it quickly into my bag. The bus arrived, and I rushed aboard, breathless. All day, I floated through school, questions swirling. Was this innocent? Dangerous? Both?

I decided to let the answers wait.

One afternoon, watching from the kitchen, I saw a Jeep pull up instead of Seud. It was Faye, his older brother. He smiled when our eyes met. Moments later, he knocked at the door—confident, charming, unmistakably present.

Where Seud's presence calmed, Faye's filled the room.

After he left, my mother seemed unsettled. "I didn't realize there were so many single men here," she said quietly.

The comment lingered.

One of my chores was watering the plants in the sunroom, visible from the floor above. One afternoon, a folded piece of paper drifted down at my feet. I looked up—Seud stood at his window. I slipped it into my pocket.

Later, alone in my room, I unfolded it. A poem about love, signed by one of my favorite composers, Darius. I hid it in my shoe, my heart pounding.

Then everything shifted again.

Coming home from school one day, I found the house empty. A knock followed. Mrs. Bonlou stood there, calm but urgent.

"Your mother has been in labor all morning," she said. "She's at the hospital."

Then softly, "Seud drove her."

At the hospital, I met my newborn brother, Bo. Despite an emergency C-section, my mother was radiant with strength. Later, as I walked toward the cafeteria, I ran into Seud again. He explained he had been repairing the hospital's air-conditioning system.

In that moment, he felt like a hero.

When my mother returned home, Mrs. Bonlou cared for her daily. She watched me closely—praising my help, hinting gently that I might be a good match for one of her sons.

Then came the dinner.

The house filled with food and laughter, but beneath it, tension pulsed. Faye's gaze lingered too long. Seud's eyes met mine just a heartbeat longer than safe. Too many coincidences. Too many near-misses.

My aunt—my mother's younger sister—knew everything. Seud often visited her. Through her home, our secret grew quietly: tea, music, dreams whispered with care.

Meanwhile, Faye worked his way into my mother's trust— attentive, patient, helpful. Flowers appeared. Conversations deepened.

Late one night, jasmine scented the air. I stood by my window under moonlight. Across from me, a brief flicker of light appeared—then vanished.

I didn't close the curtain.

I stayed where I was. Waiting. Knowing.

Something fragile and forbidden had begun.

And soon, it would demand a choice

Chapter 12
Engagement Chaos

There are moments in life when the air itself feels different—charged, uneasy—as if the universe knows something you don't. The days before everything unraveled carried that kind of stillness. Smiles felt forced. Laughter came too easily. Even sunlight seemed to linger where it shouldn't.

I didn't understand it then, but every glance and every whispered secret was another thread tightening toward the inevitable.

When it finally snapped, it didn't arrive as an explosion. It came quietly, in the ordinary glow of an afternoon—the kind of moment you don't recognize as life-altering until it already is.

It collapsed in the sunroom.

I was laughing and whispering with Seud, sunlight catching the curve of his smile, when I turned—and saw her.

My mother.

Late-afternoon light filtered through the lace curtains, scattering restless shadows across the floor. I heard the faint creak of the hallway boards—the sound that always announced her presence. Time stilled. Her face was calm, but her eyes carried a question I couldn't afford to answer.

She stepped forward, curiosity edged with authority.

"What were you doing in there?"

Her gaze sharpened. "Are you talking to that boy?"

My heart raced. I denied everything, but even as the words left my mouth, I knew she already knew. The secret I had guarded so carefully was no longer mine.

From that moment on, my mother seemed to be everywhere. Her watchfulness followed me through the house, through the day. She insisted I come straight home after school. I noticed her standing at the kitchen window, watching as I boarded the bus. She even suspected my aunt.

Visits that once felt safe now felt like traps. She questioned why my aunt didn't come to our house instead. Sometimes she sent a sibling along with me. Eventually, she confronted my aunt directly. My aunt denied everything, but by then, suspicion had already taken root.

Seud and I were reduced to glances—brief, fragile exchanges. A smile that had to hold entire conversations. My mother watched like a hawk.

By then, Faye had made his intentions clear. And my mother's frustration was unmistakable. She hadn't expected me to fall in love—especially not in a way that disrupted the future my parents had spent years planning.

One day, she confronted me directly.

"We had other plans for you," she said. Her voice trembled despite her effort to control it. "You were supposed to… never mind. You'll understand someday."

Then she said it plainly.

"I won't let you marry Seud."

The words crushed me. I ran to my room, sobbing, shouting through tears.

"I don't like Faye! This isn't fair!"

But my mother didn't soften. She told me that if I was thinking about marriage instead of education—and instead of leaving the country—it would have to be with someone older, more established.

When my father returned from his trip, his disappointment mirrored hers. Together, they made it clear: if the Bonlou family came to ask for my hand on Faye's behalf, they would agree.

I didn't yet know how much would unravel in the days ahead.

Faye knew nothing about Seud and me. Brothers like that didn't share romantic truths. But Seud knew about Faye's plans—and it broke him.

He poured his heart out to my aunt, tears in his eyes, telling her his family was preparing to ask for my hand for his brother. The thought of losing me—to his own brother—shattered him.

The Bonlou family began preparations. Mr. Bonlou gathered everyone. Their youngest son returned home from another city. When he met Seud, Seud confessed everything. The younger brother tried to drop subtle hints to Faye, but Faye dismissed them and pushed forward.

That evening, they arrived with flowers, sweets, and gifts.

I felt numb.

My heart belonged to Seud. My parents refused to listen. I couldn't stand Faye. I felt powerless—caught in a current that pulled me whether I resisted or not. And yet, a stubborn spark inside me whispered that something would shift. I didn't know how. I didn't know when. But I held on.

As night fell, tension thickened in the house. My parents' smiles were strained. Family members arrived—my aunt among them— but the warmth felt rehearsed, fragile.

I was dressed exactly as my mother instructed. My siblings were ready. The house hummed with nervous anticipation.

Then the doorbell rang.

The Bonlou family stood on the porch: Mr. and Mrs. Bonlou, Faye, and the youngest and oldest sons.

One person was missing.

Seud.

He had quietly slipped away to my aunt's house, unwilling to witness the evening. Before leaving, he bought me a gold pendant and left it there—a silent act of defiance, a farewell without words.

Inside, the request unfolded. My parents gave their blessing.

When it was my turn, emotion surged. I couldn't speak. I nodded, my heart pounding.

The engagement date was set.

Faye insisted the celebration take place the very next weekend. He rushed everything—eager, impatient. With my parents' reluctant approval, invitations were sent. A dress was purchased. Jewelry chosen.

The days leading up to it felt like walking toward a storm I couldn't escape. Every conversation tightened the air. Every silence grew heavier. My mother tracked me everywhere—not with anger, but with watchfulness.

The engagement night arrived.

Fifteen to twenty relatives filled the Bonlou home. Chandeliers glowed too brightly. Laughter sounded too loud. The scent of saffron rice and perfume thickened the air.

Seud stood quietly in a corner, his jaw clenched, his eyes shimmering. When the ring slid onto my trembling finger, silent tears traced his face.

Then Faye tightened the noose.

He brought in a mullah and announced he wanted to make the marriage official that night. My heart stopped when he asked my mother for my birth certificate.

The room froze.

Then my mother stood.

"No," she said firmly. "This is an engagement, not a marriage. There will be no certificates exchanged tonight."

The room exhaled. The mullah hesitated. Faye flushed. But my mother did not waver.

That night ended quietly.

The next morning, Mrs. Bonlou asked me to help prepare breakfast. Then she said gently, "Could you check on Grandma?" I walked down the hall and opened the door softly.

It wasn't Grandma.

It was Seud.

He looked up and whispered, "Hello, my love."

Before I could move, Faye appeared in the doorway.

"What are you two doing?" he demanded.

Seud scrambled for an explanation. It fell flat.

Moments later, Mrs. Bonlou arrived. The truth hovered—
unspoken, undeniable.

I fled.

In my room, my hands shook. My parents followed. I told them
everything.

When I finished, silence filled the space.

And in that silence, I understood something with painful clarity:

Nothing would ever be the same again.

Outside, the night remained calm and indifferent.
Inside our lives, a storm had already begun.

Chapter 13
Breaking Free

Morning light barely touched the edges of my room before the tension from the night before seeped in with it. Every sound felt amplified—the rustle of curtains, the creak of floorboards, the low hum of the refrigerator. I hadn't slept. My mind replayed Faye's confrontation again and again, each memory tightening around my chest.

Then came a gentle knock.

Mrs. Bonlou stood in the doorway, her face calm but unreadable. "Mr. Bonlou asked me to send you upstairs," she said softly.

My stomach dropped. Conversations like that never ended well.

I followed her down the hall, each step heavier than the last. Outside, Faye sat quietly, watching. Across the street, near the corner, I thought I caught a glimpse of Seud's familiar silhouette slipping out of sight. The air felt charged. Nothing felt safe or predictable anymore.

Mr. Bonlou—the head of the family—had finally sensed that something was wrong, though no one had dared tell him the whole truth. He was a man everyone respected, even feared slightly. And now he wanted answers.

Upstairs, his office door stood slightly ajar. Faye, Seud, and I sat outside in silence, like students waiting to be called in. I kept my head down, hands folded tightly in my lap, unable to look at either of them. My heart still felt bruised.

The silence stretched until Mr. Bonlou stepped out.

"I want to speak with each of you," he said evenly. "One at a time."

Faye went in first. The door closed behind him. Minutes passed slowly, thick with tension. Seud shifted beside me, glancing my way, but I couldn't meet his eyes. I just wanted it to be over.

When Faye emerged, his face was pale and unreadable. He walked past me without a word.

Then it was Seud's turn.

While Seud was inside, Faye tried to speak to me. I lifted my hand gently.

"Please," I said quietly. "Give me a moment. I don't want to talk to anyone right now—only to Mr. Bonlou."

He hesitated, then nodded and stepped away.

When Seud finally came out, his face carried the same tension he'd taken in with him. Moments later, Mr. Bonlou called my name.

74

My heart pounded as I entered his office. He stood near the window, hands clasped behind his back, morning light spilling across the desk. When he turned toward me, sadness filled his expression.

"My dear," he said, "I am devastated by what I've learned. I had no idea this was happening. But I want you to know something—I care deeply for you. I always hoped you would become part of our family. No matter which of my sons, I would have been proud to call you, my daughter-in-law."

I took a steady breath and lifted my eyes.
"Mr. Bonlou, thank you. That means more than you know. But I need to be honest."

He nodded, inviting me to continue.

"What happened yesterday made something clear to me. I never want to live with this kind of confusion again. If I marry Faye, knowing Seud loves me—and that Faye knows it—I will never find peace. And if I marry Seud, knowing Faye once wanted me, it would be the same. No matter what I choose, someone is hurt. I would always be walking on eggshells."

My voice trembled, but I didn't stop.

"I love your family. But I can't do this. This isn't anger or judgment—it's clarity. I'm asking you to support my decision and speak to my father. I know this is the right choice."

For a long moment, he said nothing. Then his expression softened.

"I cannot believe how wise and brave you are," he said quietly. "You're right. I hadn't considered how this pain would follow all of you. You have my full support. I will speak to your father. You have my word."

Relief rushed through me.

When I stepped back into the hallway, the weight on my chest eased. Seud stood nearby, anger and worry flickering across his face.

"You can't just leave like this," he whispered.

"I have to," I said, my voice unsteady but firm.

Downstairs, my parents were waiting. Their faces were tight with worry.

"What happened?" my father asked.

I told them everything. As I spoke, the tension slowly gave way to something quieter—understanding.

"You did the right thing," my mother said softly.

Later that evening, my father came into my room.

"It's done," he said. "Mr. Bonlou agrees. He'll speak to both sons. And we're moving. I canceled the lease."

For the first time in days, the silence felt peaceful.

We packed quickly. By Monday, we were gone—no goodbyes, no explanations.

The new apartment was quiet, almost unnerving. Life now existed in two layers: the visible routine of each day and the hidden urgency of preparing to leave the country.

Three days later, I saw Faye across the street.

The next morning, Seud stood there too.

My uncles began walking me to and from school. I was never alone.

Two weeks later, Faye appeared at our apartment.

He pulled a knife.

Time slowed.

"I'll go with him," I begged my father. "Please—don't let him hurt you."

My father stepped in front of me.

"Over my dead body," he said.

My uncles rushed forward. My father demanded the knife be dropped. Faye shouted about the money he had spent. Without hesitation, my father wrote a check and pressed it into his chest.

Faye left.

Only then did I realize I could breathe.

I collapsed into my father's arms.

That night, the apartment was quiet again. Boxes half-packed. Shadows stretching long across the walls.

I sat by the window; my forehead pressed against the cool glass. The street outside looked calm—but I knew better.

Freedom had been claimed.

But the cost of it was only beginning to reveal itself.

Chapter 14
Planning the Exit

Only a few weeks remained before school ended. My parents moved carefully now, guided by a plan so quiet and deliberate that even our closest relatives couldn't know. My sister and I would leave the apartment first—before anyone noticed, before questions could be asked. The house felt tense, as if every shadow were sharper and every sound louder than it should have been.

My mother's closest friend—a woman she had known for more than thirty years—lived about thirty minutes away. When my mother told her what had happened, there was no hesitation. "Bring them here tonight," she said, firm and steady—the kind of voice that could calm a storm.

That night unfolded in whispers. My mother packed our bags slowly, piece by piece, the soft rustle of clothes betraying the silence we worked so hard to protect. My father pulled the truck around to the back so no one would see us leave. Streetlights stretched our shadows across the pavement as we climbed inside. The metal door handles were cold beneath my fingers. Each heartbeat felt thunderous, echoing inside my chest like a warning.

When we arrived, warm lamplight spilled onto the driveway, offering a fragile sense of relief. Inside, lavender sachets scented the air, mingling with the comforting smell of tea and fresh bread. I brushed my hand across the soft rug, grateful for the safety, even as fear twisted in my stomach. It wasn't home—but it was shelter.

The next morning, her husband drove me to school. He knew a security guard who let me enter through a back door reserved for teachers. Each day, I slipped inside quietly, walking narrow hallways thick with shadow and chalk dust. The smell of old books grounded me in something familiar. Every step was measured. Every glance cautious.

Even that wasn't enough.

My parents knew that if word reached relatives—especially those who might not understand—everything could unravel. For decades, they had been the backbone of the family: hosting gatherings, keeping everyone connected, holding relationships together. Now, secrecy was survival.

Eight days remained.

My parents sold what they could, gave possessions to those in need, and packed with military precision. I imagined the sounds echoing through the empty apartment—the snap of tape, the clink of dishes—each noise heavy with finality.

School ended. I collected my diploma. Freedom drew closer with every silent ride, every hidden entrance, every goodbye that had to remain unspoken.

The final night at my mother's friend's house was thick with silence. Time dragged, each tick of the clock counting down to the unknown.

Morning arrived gray and still. We climbed into my father's truck and drove like soldiers into uncertainty—eyes forward, hearts pounding. Hours passed. Mountains rose ahead of us like silent witnesses. Dust and diesel stung the air as we approached the border.

The control posts stood rigid. Guards watched. Dogs barked in the distance. My palms were slick with sweat. My sister's hand trembled in mine.

And then—just like that—we crossed.

Iran fell behind us. Turkey lay ahead.

I inhaled deeply, my breath shaking. The air felt different here. Streets buzzed with life. Vendors called out. Sunlight bounced off rooftops and spires reaching skyward. Freedom whispered in every sound.

Still, the past clung to me. Memories of our apartment, familiar streets, and the scent of home lingered like ghosts. I pressed my hand against my backpack and closed my eyes for a moment— letting the weight settle before opening them to the unfamiliar world ahead.

My parents remained tense but purposeful. The truck hummed beneath us. Every glance in the rearview mirror reminded me: we were leaving, and nothing would ever be the same.

Hours later, Istanbul appeared—alive, vast, shimmering beneath the afternoon sun. The scent of roasted chestnuts and spices filled the air. My heart pounded with a fierce blend of fear, relief, and possibility.

For the first time in weeks, I breathed fully.

We were free.

That night, the truck slowed in a quiet alley far from the city's pulse. We stepped out, exhausted, hearts still racing. Shadows shifted. The town whispered around us—sirens, voices, footsteps echoing through unfamiliar streets. We had escaped danger, crossed borders, and claimed freedom.

And yet, uncertainty wrapped around me like a cloak.

Our real journey—the one that would test every ounce of courage, trust, and love we had—was only beginning.

Epilogue

I could not have known what storms or triumphs awaited me. Yet deep inside, a fierce certainty burned. The road ahead would demand everything—strip me bare, test my courage, and challenge every belief I held.

The wind tore through my hair, carrying the scent of rain and possibility. The path shimmered before me, each turn alive with secrets waiting to be revealed. Fear no longer ruled me. In its place stood something sharper. Brighter. A promise.

I lifted my chin and stepped forward.

Each step echoed with resolve. Each heartbeat pulsed with conviction. The world might threaten, tempt, or twist—but I would not falter.

This was my story.
Mine alone.

And I would claim it—fierce, unyielding, and alive.

Beyond the horizon, shadows still moved, whispering of journeys yet to come and truths still waiting to be faced. For every ending carries the seed of a beginning.

And I had only just begun.

A Note on Continuity

This book is one part of a larger life, told in stages.

What you have read is complete in itself—a beginning shaped by displacement, faith, and the first recognition that freedom has a cost. Other chapters of this life exist, unfolding across different countries, seasons, and awakenings. They are not required to understand this one.

Stories do not always end when the page does.
Some continue because life does.

Author's Note on Anonymity

This work is published anonymously by choice.

Not to hide the truth—but to protect it.

Some stories carry more than one life within them. Remaining unnamed allows this story to stand on its own, without turning lived experience into spectacle or identity into currency. The intention is not distance, but care—for those who appear in these pages, and for the reader who meets them.

Silence, when chosen consciously, can be an act of authorship.

End of Book One

The Journey Between Two Worlds

A volume in the **Freedom Price Tag** *series*